Editor
Barbara M. Wally, M.S.

Editorial Manager
Ina Massler Levin, M.A.

Editor in Chief
Sharon Coan, M.S. Ed.

Cover Artist
Sue Fullam

Art Coordinator
Cheri Macoubrie Wilson

Creative Director
Elayne Roberts

Imaging
Ralph Olmedo, Jr.

Product Manager
Phil Garcia

Publishers
Rachelle Cracchiolo, M.S. Ed.
Mary Dupuy Smith, M.S. Ed.

How to Punctuate

Grades 1–3

Author

J. L. Smith

Teacher Created Materials, Inc.
6421 Industry Way
Westminster, CA 92683
www.teachercreated.com

ISBN-1-57690-497-0

©1999 Teacher Created Materials, Inc.

Made in U.S.A.

Table of Contents

Introduction

What It Is…

How to Punctuate is a resource for your classroom. You may use the book as a workbook to teach punctuation or use individual pages to supplement activities you are already doing in your classroom.

The Basics…

Punctuation rules appropriate for grades 1–3 are presented in this book. Each page has the punctuation rule listed at the top. A brief description and examples of how to use the rule are listed for students to refer to during practice. Plenty of exercises are provided for students to practice the rule listed at the top of the page. Some concepts have only one page of practice. Other concepts have several pages of practice. It is up to the teacher to select which pages are appropriate for her class. A first grade teacher may use only the first page or two of each section. A third grade teacher may use the first page for review and select other pages for continued learning.

Assessment…

Each section of the book is followed by several pages that can be used for assessment purposes. The assessments at the end of each section evaluate only the concepts covered in that section. The assessments at the end of the book cover many concepts covered throughout the book. Most assessments have two options. Again, this provides for teacher choice. The first assessment is usually shorter and asks students to identify and correct punctuation errors on a line-by-line basis. The second assessment usually asks the student to copy a paragraph, correcting any punctuation errors. A student self-assessment is provided at the end of the book for students to reflect on the things learned throughout the unit.

Additional Resources…

In addition, a handy punctuation reference sheet is provided for you on page 44. This sheet can be copied and distributed for each student in the class to keep in his notebook, or the teacher can use it as a personal reference. Posters which list the punctuation rules covered in this book are provided on pages 45–46. Again, these posters can be distributed to the students as references or can be enlarged and displayed on the wall as reminders of punctuation rules. An answer key for each of the practice exercises in the book is provided.

Endings Count

Punctuation Rule: Sentences end with punctuation marks.

How do you know when a sentence has ended and another sentence has begun? One clue we have is that an ending punctuation mark is at the end of the sentence. Another clue is that the new sentence begins with a capital letter. Imagine if sentences did not have ending punctuation marks or capital letters at the beginning. They would look like this:

> have you ever had a pet I didn't until my lucky day one sunny day I decided to play in the backyard all of a sudden I saw a lizard he ran to a shady spot behind a rock I decided to catch him I slowly walked toward the rock then I quickly cupped my hands around him I decided to keep him as a pet

This paragraph is very hard to read because there are no ending punctuation marks. Now, read the paragraph again with the punctuation marks and capital letters in it.

> Have you ever had a pet? I didn't until my lucky day. One sunny day, I decided to play in the backyard. All of a sudden, I saw a lizard. He ran to a shady spot behind a rock. I decided to catch him. I slowly walked toward the rock. Then, I quickly cupped my hands around him. I decided to keep him as a pet.

The second paragraph is much easier to read because the ending punctuation marks tell us when the sentences have ended. There are three types of ending punctuation we can use to end sentences: the period (.), the question mark (**?**), and the exclamation point (**!**).

Circle the ending punctuation mark in each sentence below.

1. The name of our team is the Bull Dogs.
2. We are the best baseball team in the city.
3. Have you ever been on a baseball team?
4. The game was tied until the last inning.
5. Do you think that we will win?
6. We won!

Tell It Like It Is

Punctuation Rule: Sentences end with punctuation marks.
Declarative *(telling)* sentences end with periods.

Every sentence needs an ending punctuation mark. A declarative sentence ends with a period. Declarative sentences are telling sentences. They tell you something.

Examples:

My brother is two years old.   I love chocolate ice cream.

When you write a declarative sentence, you need to end your sentence with a period.

Practice writing a period at the ends of these declarative sentences.

1. My family has a pet dog
2. I watched cartoons on Saturday
3. We had pizza for dinner
4. Tim rides a blue bike
5. I know a lot about dinosaurs
6. Mom asked me to help her clean
7. The hamster got out of his cage
8. I wrote a letter to my grandma

Now it is your turn. Write your own telling sentences on the lines below. Use periods at the ends.

1. _____

_____

_____

2. _____

_____

_____

End It with a Period

> **Punctuation Rule:** Sentences end with punctuation marks.
> Declarative (telling) sentences end with periods.
> Imperative sentences end with periods.

Write a declarative (telling) sentence about the picture in each box. Be sure to end each sentence with a period.

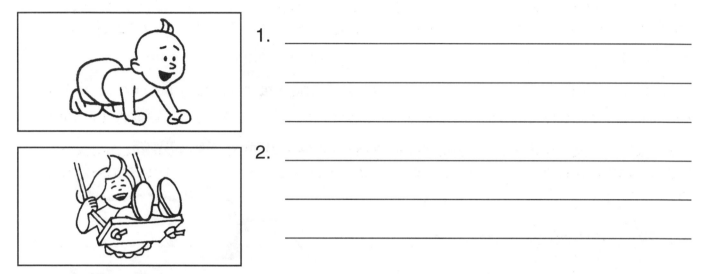

1. _____

   _____

   _____

2. _____

   _____

There is another type of sentence that ends with a period. Imperative sentences are sentences that give commands or request something. These sentences also end with a period.

Examples:

   Give me that. Run to the fence and back.

Practice ending each of these imperative sentences with a period. Rewrite each sentence on the line. Add a period to the end of each sentence.

1. Turn to page 20 _____

2. Come here _____

3. Sit down _____

Who, What, Where, Why, When

Punctuation Rule: Sentences end with punctuation marks. Interrogative (questioning) sentences end with question marks.

Do you like your dinner? Did you finish your homework? Did you have fun? These are questions you are probably asked each and every day. Interrogative sentences ask questions. Sentences that ask questions end with question marks. Look at the sentence below. The question mark is at the end of the sentence.

How old are you?

Questions usually begin with the words who, what, where, why, when, or how.

Look at the interrogative (questioning) sentences below. Circle the question mark at the end of each sentence. Then write the first word in the sentence on the line.

1. What do you want for lunch? _____

2. Where do you want to go for vacation? _____

3. Who was with you? _____

4. Is your birthday in May? _____

5. Why didn't you call me? _____

6. How did you do on your spelling test? _____

7. Do you want a snack? _____

8. When does the movie begin? _____

Extension: Did you notice the types of words that the sentences begin with? News reporters ask questions beginning with who, what, where, why, and when in order get the full story. They are called "The Five Ws." Read a newspaper article. See if you can find The Five Ws. Write the questions and the answers on the back of this paper.

Asking Questions

> **Punctuation Rule:** Sentences end with punctuation marks. Interrogative (questioning) sentences end with question marks.

Practice using question marks at the ends of interrogative sentences by writing questions. Write a question that begins with the word listed on each line. Be sure to end each sentence with a question mark. The first one has been done for you.

1. Who   is at the door? _____

2. What _____

3. Where _____

4. Why _____

5. When _____

6. Will _____

7. Can _____

8. How _____

Extension: Most questions begin with who, what, where, why, when, and how. Of course, there are other words that can begin questions. Can you think of any more? Write them on the back of this paper.

Answer It with a Question

Punctuation Rule: Sentences end with punctuation marks. Interrogative (questioning) sentences end with question marks.

You are asked hundreds of questions every day. You also ask hundreds of questions every day. Each time you write down a question, you must remember to use a question mark at the end of the sentence. Can you remember to do that? I'm sure you can.

Have you heard of the game Jeopardy? In that game, a player has to make up a question to match the answer. Practice writing questions for the following answers. Have fun. The questions can be as silly or as serious as you want them to be. Be sure to end each sentence with a question mark. The first one has been done for you.

Question	**Answer**
1. What did I dream about last night?	a big green monster
2. _____	hot dogs
3. _____	three
4. _____	August
5. _____	cartoons
6. _____	math
7. _____	sisters
8. _____	purple
9. _____	pretzels and orange juice
10. _____	red, white, and blue

Extension: On the back of this paper, write down two questions that you asked today.

Show Emotion!

> **Punctuation Rule:** Sentences end with punctuation marks.
> Exclamatory sentences end with exclamation pointa.

Exclamatory sentences show strong emotions or feelings. Usually these sentences tell something (like declarative sentences) or give commands (like imperative sentences), but the writer wants the reader to know that the sentence is being said with strong emotion. The writer uses an exclamation point at the end of the sentence, instead of a period, to show the emotion.

Exclamatory sentences usually look and sound like this:

Watch out! We won the game!

When you read these sentences, read them with excitement in your voice. Your voice can show the emotion that the exclamation point conveys.

Write an exclamation point at the end of each sentence below. Then read each sentence, showing the emotion the sentence has by the tone of your voice.

1. We're done with school

2. The movie was great

3. Drop it

4. Be careful

5. I did it

6. Get me out of here

7. I finished

8. The lizard escaped

9. I passed the test

10. Look out for the fire

Each sentence above could end with a period instead of an exclamation point. How would the sentence change if you put a period at the end of each sentence? Read each sentence as if there were a period at the end.

Extension: Think of two exclamatory sentences you used today. **Hint:** You probably use a lot of exclamatory sentences on the playground at recess.

Another Use for an Exclamation Point

Punctuation Rule: Sentences end with punctuation marks.
Use an exclamation point after an interjection.

Hey! Yikes! Look out! Did you know that these types of words are a part of speech called interjections? An interjection shows a strong emotion and usually ends with an exclamation point. Often there is a sentence that follows the interjection. Sometimes the sentences that follow end with periods. Other times, if the emotion is still strong, the following sentence ends with another exclamation point. Here are some examples.

Ouch! That was hot! Thanks! I really needed a new bike.

In both sentences, the interjections "ouch" and "thanks" show strong emotions. They are each followed by an exclamation point. In the first example, "That was hot!" still shows strong emotion. That sentence ends with another exclamation point. The second example, "I really needed a new bike," does not need to show as much emotion. It is fine to end that sentence with a period.

Choose four words from the box below. Use each word as an interjection. Then write a sentence to follow the interjection. You can use either a period or an exclamation point to end your sentence. You decide how much emotion you want to show.

Interjections

Ouch	Hey	Help	Aha	Yuck	Look out	Yes
Thanks	Yikes	Wow	Oops	Hooray	Phew	No

---

1. _____

2. _____

3. _____

4. _____

Abbreviate It

> **Punctuation Rule:** Use a period after most abbreviations.

An abbreviation is a short way to write a word. For example, you can use *ft.* to abbreviate the word *foot*. Notice the period that follows the letters *ft. Mar.* is an abbreviation for the word *March*. A period is used after most abbreviations.

Put a period after each abbreviation below. Then match each abbreviation to the word it abbreviates.

Abbreviations	Words
1. Mar	street
2. Tues	yard
3. yr	inch
4. ft	Tuesday
5. doz	Doctor
6. Dr	Junior
7. pg	year
8. ave	avenue
9. Jr	page
10. yd	March
11. in	feet
12. St	dozen

You may have noticed that the punctuation rule said that most abbreviations have periods after them. That is because there are some abbreviations that are not followed by periods. The list below shows some abbreviations that do not have periods after them.

Abbreviations Not Followed by Periods

asap—as soon as possible	km—kilometer
ht—height	g—gram
C—Celsius	ml—mililiter
kg—kilogram	F—Fahrenheit
cm—centimeter	mph—miles per hour

12

Shortened Names

Punctuation Rule: Use a period after most abbreviations.

You just learned that an abbreviation is a short way to write a word. Did you know that you can abbreviate your name? When you write only the first letter of your name, it is an abbreviation. This is a special abbreviation called an initial. You can write the initials of your first, middle, and last names. Here is how it looks:

If your name is Neil John Thomas, you can write your initials any one of these ways:

N. John Thomas,   N. J. Thomas,   Neil J. Thomas,   N. J. T.

Notice that each time a letter is omitted from a name, a period is put in the letter's place. A period is used after an initial that abbreviates a name.

Practice abbreviating the names below by writing the initials. You can choose which name(s) you want to abbreviate.

1. Sarah Jane Willson _____

2. Michael David Mayer _____

3. Jennifer Lynn Thore _____

4. Brittany Nicole Adams _____

Try abbreviating this famous name. John Jacob Jingleheimer Schmidt

_____

Now it is your turn to abbreviate your name. Write your full name on the line below. Then write an abbreviation of your name.

_____

_____

Extension: Try abbreviating some of your friends' names. Write their full names and their initials on the back of this paper.

Leaving Things Out

> **Punctuation Rule:** Use an ellipsis to show where words have been left out of a text.

An ellipsis can be helpful if you want to copy a text but you don't want to write the whole thing. You can write down part of the text and then use an ellipsis to show where you have left out words. An ellipsis is three periods (. . .) in a row.

Example: "The school welcomed twelve students from Canada who were visiting the U.S."

"The ceremony honored twelve students . . . visiting the U.S."

The words "from Canada who were" have been left out of the second sentence.

An ellipsis can be used in places where the reader will know what is being left out or if what is left out does not matter.

An ellipsis can also be used to show a pause in the flow of a sentence. It is especially useful in quoting a person's speech.

Sam thought and thought . . . and then thought some more. "I'm wondering. . . ."

The three periods do not replace the period at the end of a sentence. If the ellipsis comes at the end of a sentence, the ellipsis will be placed after the period (. . . .), making a total of four dots.

Try using an ellipsis in the following examples. Rewrite the text on the line under each example. Leave out the part of the text that is in parenthesis.

1. Jack, be nimble; (Jack, be quick; Jack,) jump over the candlestick.

_____

_____

2. Jack and Jill went up the hill, (To fetch a pail of water); Jack fell down, (and broke his crown, And) Jill came tumbling after.

_____

_____

3. Mary had a little lamb, (Its fleece was white as snow), And everywhere that Mary went, (The lamb was sure to go.)

_____

_____

Ending Punctuation Assessment

Option 1

Decide whether the ending punctuation mark on each sentence below needs to be a period, question mark, or exclamation point. Then write the correct punctuation mark at the end of the sentence.

1. Are you going to come with us _____

2. My mom will pick us up from school _____

3. Joey gave me a piece of gum _____

4. I won _____

5. Her favorite color is green _____

6. What should I eat for lunch _____

7. That is expensive _____

8. I need to clean my hamster's cage _____

9. What are we going to play at recess _____

10. I got an A _____

Bonus: On the line next to each sentence, write down what type of sentence it is. Write the word declarative, interrogative, imperative, or exclamatory.

Ending Punctuation Assessment

Option 2

Write a sentence for each type of ending punctuation mark.

1. period

   _____

2. question mark

   _____

3. exclamation point

   _____

4. exclamation point used after an interjection

   _____

Write the abbreviation for each of the following:

5. doctor

   _____

6. street

   _____

7. feet

   _____

8. Monday

   _____

9. dozen

   _____

10. page

    _____

Write your complete name.

_____

Write an abbreviation for your name.

_____

Listing Items

Punctuation Rule: Use commas to separate items in a series

Do you like chocolate, vanilla, or strawberry ice cream? When you list items in a row, like the flavors of ice cream, use commas to separate the items. The commas help the reader read the list with more ease. Read the same sentence without any commas. Do you like chocolate vanilla or strawberry ice cream? Don't you think that the first sentence was easier to read?

Look at how commas are used in these sentences.

Examples:

I brought gum for Mandy, Sarah, and Lin.

I like dogs, cats, and birds.

Each box below has pictures of three items. List the items in the box in a series. Be sure to separate each item with a comma. The first one has been done for you.

1. pencil, pen, and paper _____

2. _____

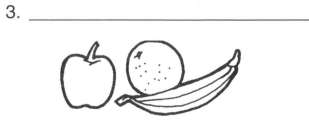

3. _____

4. _____

5. _____

6. _____

Separating Words in a Series

Punctuation Rule: Use commas to separate words in a series.

Each sentence below contains words listed in a series. Practice using commas to separate the words in each series.

1. I had a sandwich a banana and cookies for lunch.

2. Is your favorite color blue yellow or red?

3. We saw clowns acrobats and elephants at the circus.

4. I like to play soccer baseball and hockey.

5. Would you like to use crayons markers or pencils to color the picture?

6. Do you want to draw color or paint?

7. We went on field trips to the farm museum and fire station.

8. Do you want to be a policeman fireman or teacher when you grow up?

9. Tom Neil Emma Chad and Sam each gave me a birthday present.

10. We can have pizza chicken hamburgers or spaghetti for dinner.

Extension: Make your own lists. Be sure to separate the items in each list by using a comma.

My Favorite Things

> **Punctuation Rule:** Use commas to separate words in a series.

Practice using commas in series by answering the questions below. Be sure each answer is in a complete sentence. The first one has been done for you.

1. What are your three favorite colors?

   <u>Yellow, blue, and red are my three favorite colors.</u>

2. What are your four favorite foods?

   _____

3. What are your four favorite animals?

   _____

4. What are your three favorite subjects in school?

   _____

5. When you grown up, what are three jobs you might like to have?

   _____

6. What are your four favorite fruits or vegetables?

   _____

7. What are the names of your three best friends?

   _____

A New, Exciting Use for Commas

Punctuation Rule: Use commas to separate adjectives describing the same noun.

Commas are also used to separate describing words, or adjectives. Use commas to separate adjectives when they describe the same noun.

Examples:

The friendly, furry, brown dog wagged his tail.

The clown had long, red, frizzy hair.

Separate the adjectives in the sentences below by putting commas in the correct places.

1. My dog has a wet pink tongue.

2. Juanita brought a sharp new yellow pencil to school.

3. A big new shiny car raced past us.

4. The big hairy green monster scared me.

5. We play handball with the big bouncy red ball.

6. My sister wore old torn jeans.

7. I like to eat juicy sweet red apples.

8. The large hot pepperoni pizza was delivered to our house.

9. A tall bald man knocked on the door.

10. My dad has a long dark fuzzy mustache.

Extension: Think of two adjectives to describe the word toy. Then turn this paper over and write a sentence using the word toy and the two adjectives.

Describing Nouns

Punctuation Rule: Use commas to separate adjectives describing the same noun.

Complete each sentence by writing at least two adjectives in each blank. Remember to separate adjectives with commas.

1. The _____ road made me carsick.

2. My _____ teacher assigns a lot of homework.

3. The baby had _____ hair.

4. Her _____ bike was fun to ride.

5. We had fun dancing to the _____ music.

6. The _____ coat was warm.

Now it's your turn. Try writing your own sentences using the adjectives and nouns below.

1. bouncy, red ball

_____

2. slimy, green frog

_____

3. tall, skinny man

_____

4. soft, white kitten

_____

Writing the Date

> **Punctuation Rule:** Use a comma to separate the day and year when writing a date.

When writing a date, use a comma to separate the day from the year. If the date you are writing is the month of March, the 21st day, and the year 1465, you would write it to look like this: March 21, 1465.

In the United States, we write the name of the month first, followed by the day of the month, and then the year. A comma is used to separate the numbers in the day from the numbers in the year. The comma makes the date easier to read.

Write today's date on the line below. Then practice writing a comma between the day and the year by rewriting the dates listed below.

Today's date is _____.

Month	Day	Year	Month, Day, and Year
March	2	1962	March 2, 1962
1. April	15	2007	
2. December	31	1835	
3. February	3	2010	
4. August	10	1987	

You can also abbreviate the month when writing the date. In that case, you need a period after the abbreviation and a comma after the day and before the year.

Example: Jan. 15, 2001

In the following dates, the month is abbreviated. Rewrite each one, placing a period after the abbreviation and a comma after the day.

5. Feb 11 1929 _____   6. Apr 8 2000 _____

7. Mar 16 2003 _____   8. Sept 21 1997 _____

Extension: Many other countries, and some government offices, use a different order for the month, day, and year. Find out in what other order the date can be written.

Special Dates — Holidays

> **Punctuation Rule:** Use a comma to separate the day and year when writing a date.

Dates are closely associated with holidays. Some holidays are held on the same date every year. For example, Valentine's Day is always on February 14. It does not matter on what day of the week the 14th occurs.

Listed below are the dates of some holidays that occur on the same day each year. Practice separating the day from the year by adding a comma to each date and writing the current year.

New Year's Day	January 1 _____
Valentine's Day	February 14 _____
St. Patrick's Day	March 17 _____
April Fool's Day	April 1 _____
Earth Day	April 22 _____
Cinco de Mayo	May 5 _____
Halloween	October 31 _____
Veterans Day	November 11 _____
Christmas	December 25 _____
New Year's Eve	December 31 _____

Not all holidays are on the same date every year. Holidays such as Thanksgiving are on the same day of the week. Thanksgiving is always held the fourth Thursday of November. The date changes from year to year.

Look on a calendar to find out the date that each of the following holidays will be on this year. Write the date on the line next to each holiday.

Presidents' Day	February _____
Easter	(March or April) _____
Mother's Day	May _____
Father's Day	June _____
Labor Day	September _____
Columbus Day	October _____
Thanksgiving	November _____
Hanukkah	(November or December) _____

Extension: On the back of this paper, write about another holiday you observe. Be sure to include the date if you know it.

Cities and States

> **Punctuation Rule:** Use a comma to separate the city and state when writing them together.

A comma is used to separate the city from the state when you write them together. If you live in the city of Albany in the state of New York, you would write it like this: Albany, New York. Usually you write the name of the city and then the name of the state. A comma is used in between.

Practice placing a comma between the city and state. Complete the chart below by writing the city and the state together in the last column. Remember to put a comma between the city and state.

City	State	City, State
1. Boston	Massachusetts	
2. Eden Prairie	Minnesota	
3. San Francisco	California	
4. Tempe	Arizona	
5. Roanoke	Virginia	
6. Detroit	Michigan	
7. Orlando	Florida	
8. Youngstown	Ohio	

You use a comma between the city and state even if you abbreviate the state. For example, if you sent a letter to Sioux City, Iowa, you would use an abbreviation for the state. It would look like this:

Sioux City, IA

Rewrite the following cities and state abbreviations, separating each with a comma.

9.   Anchorage   AK   _____

10.   Boise   ID   _____

11.   Newark   NJ   _____

12.   Baltimore   MD   _____

Addressing an Envelope

Punctuation Rule: Use a comma to separate the city and state when writing them together.

A common place you have to write the city and state together is when you write an address on an envelope. The post office uses the information you write in order to deliver the envelope. Below is a sample of how to address an envelope. Notice where the city and state are placed on the envelope.

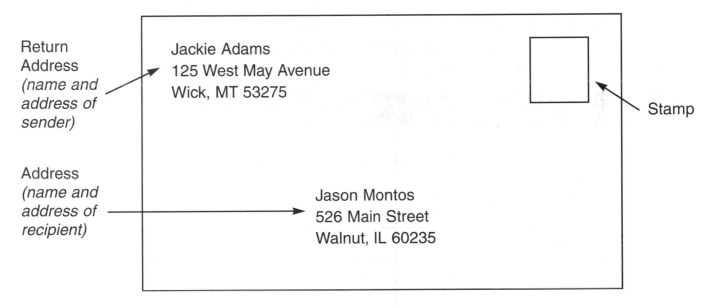

Return Address *(name and address of sender)*

Jackie Adams
125 West May Avenue
Wick, MT 53275

Stamp

Address *(name and address of recipient)*

Jason Montos
526 Main Street
Walnut, IL 60235

Now it is your turn. Use your name and address or make up a name and address in order to address the envelope below. You can add a stamp design of your own creation.

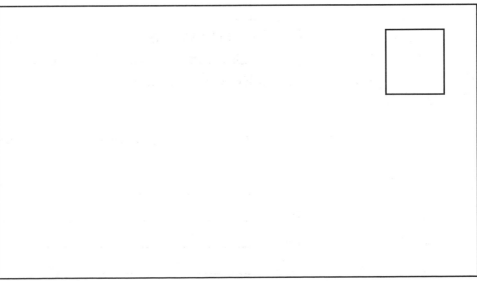

Writing to a Friend

Punctuation Rule: Use a comma after the greeting and closing in a letter.

Have you ever received a letter? Most letters from a friend follow the format of a friendly letter. These letters are less formal than a business letter and usually begin: Dear _____. After the word "dear" comes the name of the person to whom you are writing. This is called the greeting. A comma follows the name. Look at the format of the friendly letter below. Notice that a comma follows the greeting.

Date ————————▶	January 7, 2000
Greeting ————————▶	Dear Sam,
Body ————————▶	I am writing to thank you for inviting me to your house on Saturday. I had a lot of fun playing with you and all the new toys you received for your birthday. Lunch was delicious. Your mom makes the best grilled cheese sandwiches in town. I hope that you will be able to come to my house to play some day soon.
Closing ————————————————————▶	Love, Joe

Notice that there is another comma after the word "Love" at the end of the letter. This is called the closing. A closing remark is made at the end of the letter, followed by the name of the person who wrote the letter. Use a comma to separate the closing from the name.

Practice placing commas after the following greetings and closings. Add a person's name to the greeting.

1. Respectfully
2. Sincerely
3. Best wishes
4. With love

5. Dear
6. Yours truly
7. Sincerely yours
8. Love

A Friendly Letter

Punctuation Rule: Use a comma after the greeting and closing in a letter.

Practice placing a comma after the greeting and closing in a letter by writing a letter to your friend, telling her about your new hamster. Be sure to place a comma after the greeting and closing.

_____
(Date)

_____
(Greeting)

_____

_____

_____

_____

_____

_____

_____

_____

_____

_____
(Closing)

_____
(Signature)

Extension: Research the format of a business letter. Practice writing a business letter. What is the same and different about friendly and business letter punctuation?

Comma Assessment

Option 1

Correct the following sentences by adding commas and periods where they are needed.

1. My brother was born in Denver Colorado.

2. He was born on December 10 1985.

3. It was a cold windy day.

4. He weighed 7 lbs 6 oz and was a beautiful baby.

5. My parents named him Alex Jason Solas or A J for short.

6. My grandma grandpa aunt and uncle came to see him in the hospital.

7. We brought him to our house at 525 Main St after a day in the hospital.

8. He needed a lot of tender loving care.

9. He also needed lots of blankets food and diapers.

10. He started to walk on November 2 1986.

11. We cheered when A J finally walked.

Comma Assessment

Option 2

There are commas missing in various places in the letter below. Show what you know about commas by correcting the letter. Add a comma in each place where one belongs.

April 25 _____

Dear Mark

I am writing to invite you to my birthday party. There will be games food and cake. I invited all of our friends too. Mark Cathy Kevin and Sam already told me they can come. The information for the party is below.

Location: Jason L. Jones
                    452 Main St.
                    Watertown Illinois 60257

Date: May 7 _____

I will be celebrating my sixth birthday this year. I hope you can come. It will be a dull boring party without you.

                                                        Love

                                                        Jason

---

How many commas did you add to the letter? Write the number here. _____

Name five reasons you needed to add commas.

1. _____
2. _____
3. _____
4. _____
5. _____

Note to the teacher: Write the current year in the two blanks before you copy the assessment.

What Time Is It?

> **Punctuation Rule:** Use a colon to separate the hours and minutes when writing the time.

Digital clocks show the time, using only numbers. Instead of writing the words six o'clock or 6 o'clock, we can write the numbers 6:00. Six-thirty is written 6:30. A colon is used to separate the hour from the minutes when we use numbers to write the time.

colon

hour ⟶ **6:30** ⟵ minutes

Write the digital time so that it matches the time shown.

1. five o'clock

2. 7 o'clock

3. ten o'clock

_____

4. two-thirty

5. nine-thirty

6. eleven-thirty

_____

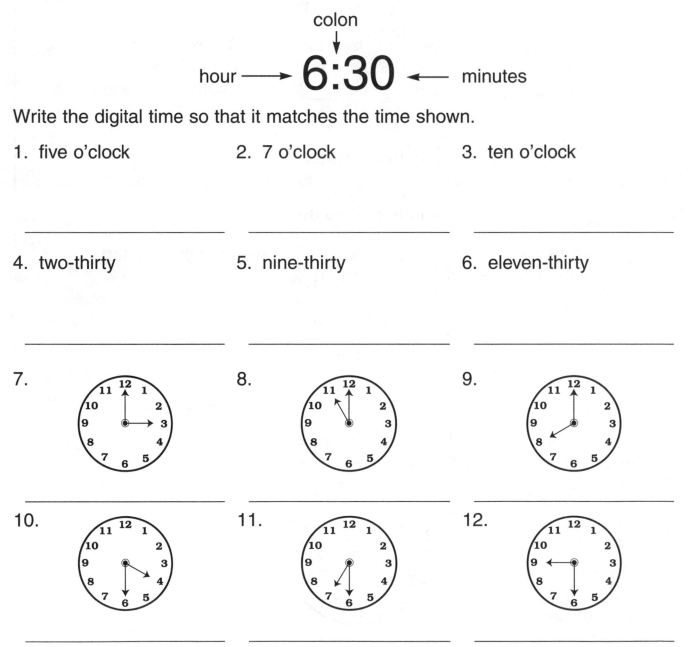

7.

8.

9.

10.

11.

12.

Be Punctual!

> **Punctuation Rule:** Use a colon to separate the hours and minutes when writing the time.

The time can be written many different ways. Sometimes time is written with only words: two-fifteen. Other times we use numbers to write the time. The time two-fifteen can also be written 2:15. A colon is used to separate the hour from the minutes when we use numbers to write the time. In the example of 2:15, the number 2 on the left of the colon is the hour. The 15 on the right of the colon shows the minutes. Take a closer look.

There are always two numbers on the minutes side of the colon. If the time is five minutes after three o'clock, you would write 3:05, not 3:5.

Practice using a colon to separate the hours and minutes by using numbers to write the times listed below.

1. 2 hours 14 minutes _____

2. 5 hours 45 minutes _____

3. 12 hours 15 minutes _____

4. 2 hours 6 minutes _____

5. 7 hours 55 minutes _____

6. 9 hours 50 minutes _____

7. _____ 8. _____ 9. _____

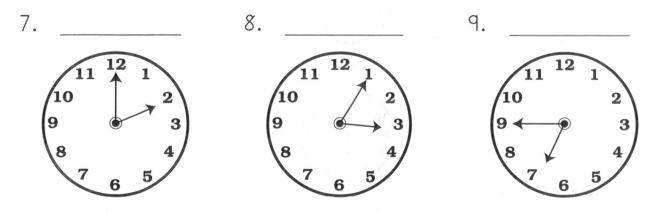

Word Munch

Punctuation Rule: Use an apostrophe when forming a contraction.

A contraction is two words combined together to form one word. Let's see how it's done.

I + will = I'll   I + am = I'm   it + is = it's   they + have = they've

In each example, the contraction combines the first word and part of the second word. One or more letters are left out in forming the contraction. An apostrophe takes the place of the letters that were left out.

Write the contraction on the line next to each set of words. Use the word bank to help you spell the contraction correctly.

Word Bank			
you're	aren't	isn't	who's
hasn't	you'll	she'll	they've
he's	we're	let's	here's

1. is + not = _____

2. let + us = _____

3. you + will = _____

4. we + are = _____

5. they + have = _____

6. are + not = _____

7. who + is = _____

8. he + is = _____

9. she + will = _____

10. you + are = _____

11. has + not = _____

12. here + is = _____

Some other common contractions follow:

I + have = I've	cannot = can't	will + not = won't
we + are = we're	did + not = didn't	is + not = isn't
they + are = they're	were + not = weren't	I + had = I'd
that + will = that'll	would + not = wouldn't	

Extension: Write five sentences on the back of this paper, using the contractions listed above.

Contraction Match

> **Punctuation Rule:** Use an apostrophe when forming a contraction.

Place an apostrophe in the contractions below. Then match each contraction to the words that are used to form the contraction. Write the letters of the words for the contractions in the spaces.

Contractions	**Words**
1. theyre _____	a. I have
2. didnt _____	b. will not
3. Ive _____	c. cannot
4. Im _____	d. I had
5. youre _____	e. she is
6. wouldnt _____	f. I will
7. lets _____	g. here is
8. shes _____	h. you are
9. were _____	i. did not
10. heres _____	j. we are
11. mustnt _____	k. let us
12. cant _____	l. I am
13. Ill _____	m. must not
14. wont _____	n. would not
15. Id _____	o. they are

Contraction Action

Punctuation Rule: Use an apostrophe when forming a contraction.

Remember that a contraction is a shorter way of saying two words. An apostrophe is used in place of the letter(s) not included in the contraction.

Rewrite each sentence below. Write a contraction in place of the underlined words.

1. *I am* going to the library.

   _____

2. *She is* going to come with me.

   _____

3. *We are* going to look for books about dinosaurs.

   _____

4. *Let us* ask for help.

   _____

5. *She will* surely help us

   _____

6. *We have* found the perfect book.

   _____

7. *It is* about the types of dinosaurs.

   _____

8. I *must have* forgotten my library card.

   _____

9. *I will* have to ask you to check it out for me.

   _____

10. I promise *it will* be turned in on time.

   _____

Extension: On the back of this paper, write about the types of books you like to check out from the library. See if you can use a contraction or two in your sentences.

That's Mine!

Punctuation Rule: Use an apostrophe to show possession.

When a word shows that something belongs to it, it shows ownership. Possession is another word for ownership. An apostrophe is used to show possession.

Example: Friskie's leash (To whom does the leash belong? The leash belongs to the dog, Friskie.) You usually add **'s** to a word to show possession.

Add an apostrophe to show ownership in the following examples.

1. the girls doll
2. the elephants trunk
3. Toms shoes
4. moms dinner
5. Sams sister
6. the principals office
7. the dogs tail
8. Jakes backpack
9. dads lawn mower
10. the childrens room

Show possession in the following examples. Don't forget the apostrophe.

1. food belonging to a cat _____

2. a nest belonging to a bird_____

3. a bike belonging to Miguel _____

4. a store that is owned by Kim _____

5. a CD player belonging to David _____

6. a book belonging to my sister _____

7. a skateboard belonging to my brother _____

8. some toys that belong to a baby _____

Showing Possession

Punctuation Rule: Use an apostrophe to show possession.

Rewrite each sentence below, adding an apostrophe where one is needed to show possession.

1. Nicky ran screaming into Manuels house. _____

   _____

2. My dad knocked down a hornets nest. _____

   _____

3. I wish I could ride my brothers bike. _____

   _____

4. An alien ate Marielas homework. _____

   _____

5. Grandpas spaghetti is the best in the world. _____

   _____

Write your own sentence showing possession for each example below.

1. a bedroom belonging to my sister _____

   _____

2. a pencil belonging to a student _____

   _____

3. hair belonging to a girl _____

   _____

4. a house belonging to the man _____

   _____

5. a nose belonging to a clown _____

   _____

What Did You Say?

Punctuation Rule: Use quotation marks around a direct quote.
Use a comma to set off a quotation.

Quotation marks are used to show the words a person is saying.

Example:

Mary said, "I love the color blue."

The words inside the quotation marks show the exact words Mary said. Notice that a comma is used to separate what Mary said from the rest of the sentence.

Place a comma and quotation marks in each sentence below.

1. The doctor said You are in good health.

2. Marty said My lizard escaped from the cage.

3. He said You look nice today.

4. Mrs. Thomas said Line up at the door.

5. Dad said Come in for dinner.

The word *said* is not the only word used to show that a person is speaking. Other words that can show a person is speaking are *asked, screamed, questioned, wondered, yelled,* and *whispered.*

Place a comma and quotation marks in each sentence below.

6. Michael asked Can I have a glass of milk?

7. Watch out! screamed Judy.

8. Jason wondered Should I go with them?

9. My sister whispered Is the movie almost over?

10. Mom yelled Go, Wildcats, go!

Who Said It?

Punctuation Rule: Use quotation marks around a direct quote.
Use a comma to set off a quotation.

Practice using quotation marks and commas by selecting a sentence from the Sentence Bank to complete each blank. You can make the sentences as serious or as silly as you want.

Sentence Bank

You will need another shot.   Let's play soccer.

Can I come along?   It's time for lunch.

Hurry up!   Don't wake the baby.

Turn to page four in your history book.   How tall will I grow?

Do pigs fly?   We won!

1. Marsha screamed _____

2. I wondered _____

3. _____ whispered Nicole.

4. She yelled _____

5. _____ asked my brother.

6. The teacher said _____

7. Mom shouted _____

8. My sister asked _____ .

Articles, Chapters, Songs, and Poems

Punctuation Rule: Use quotation marks around the titles of magazine
and newspaper articles.
Use quotation marks around chapter titles, songs,
and poem titles.

Quotation marks are used to show the title of a magazine article or a newspaper article. The quotation marks are used to set apart the title from the rest of the sentence.

Example:

There was an interesting article called "Weird Weather" in the paper today.

Quotation marks are also used around the names of chapter titles, songs, and poem titles.

Examples:

Have you read "An Explosion" in *Charlotte's Web*?
My class sang "Frere Jacques."
My favorite poem is "Boa Constrictor" by Shel Silverstein.

Practice placing quotation marks in the correct places in the sentences below.

1. Are you going to read the chapter called The Problem?

2. We sang a song to the tune of Old MacDonald Had a Farm.

3. A. A. Milne wrote a poem called The End.

4. I read an article called The Octopus.

Answer the following by writing complete sentences. Be sure to use quotation marks if you need them.

1. Name a song you know by heart. _____

_____

2. Name a poem you have read recently._____

_____

3. Name an article from a magazine or newspaper. _____

_____

Colons, Apostrophes, and Quotation Marks Assessment

Place colons, apostrophes, or quotation marks where they are needed in the examples below.

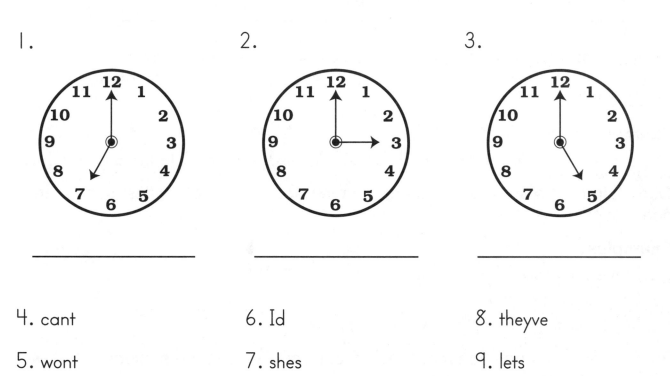

1. _____

2. _____

3. _____

4. cant

5. wont

6. Id

7. shes

8. theyve

9. lets

10. My sister screamed, Its time to come in for dinner.

11. My family eats dinner at 6 00.

12. Mom said, I made corn dogs for dinner.

13. Theyre my favorite.

14. Moms dinners are the best.

15. Maybe Ill be as good a cook as Mom when I grow up.

Unit Assessment

Option 1

Place the correct punctuation where it is needed.

Ending Punctuation

1. I went to see a movie on Saturday

2. Wow You did a good job

3. How old are you

4. Sarah finished her homework

Abbreviations

5. Dr Watson gave me medicine.

6. 12953 Main St is my address.

Commas

7. Mom bought apples bananas and pears at the grocery store.

8. I brought scissors crayons and a ruler to school.

9. The furry white rabbit ate a carrot.

10. I flew to Chicago Illinois on March 20 1998.

Colons

11. My bedtime is 8 30.

12. Our lunchtime is 12 00.

Apostrophes

13. I dont know how to play football.

14. Were ready to go.

15. Lets get popcorn to eat during the movie.

Unit Assessment

Option 2

Rewrite the following paragraph, correcting any punctuation errors.

The Three Little Pigs

Once upon a time there were three little pigs and a big bad wolf. The three little pigs built their houses out of straw sticks and bricks. After the houses were built, the wolf went to the pigs house that was made out of straw and said Little pig, little pig, let me in. The pig answered Not by the hair of my chinny chin chin. The wolf responded Then Ill huff and Ill puff and Ill blow your house down. And that is what he did. The house fell down, and the pig ran to his brothers house that was made out of sticks. The wolf went to the pigs house that was made out of sticks and yelled Little pig, little pig, let me in. The pig responded Not by the hair of my chinny chin chin. The wolf once again said Then Ill huff and Ill puff and Ill blow your house down. And that is what he did. The house fell down, and the two pigs ran to their brothers house that was made out of bricks. The wolf followed them and said Little pig, little pig, let me in. The pig responded Not by the hair of my chinny chin chin. The wolf screamed Then Ill huff and Ill puff and Ill blow your house down. And he tried to blow the house down, but it wouldnt fall. The wolf made a plan to get into the pigs house by climbing through the chimney. When he finally squeezed down the chimney, he fell into a pot and was cooked for dinner. The three little pigs lived happily ever after.

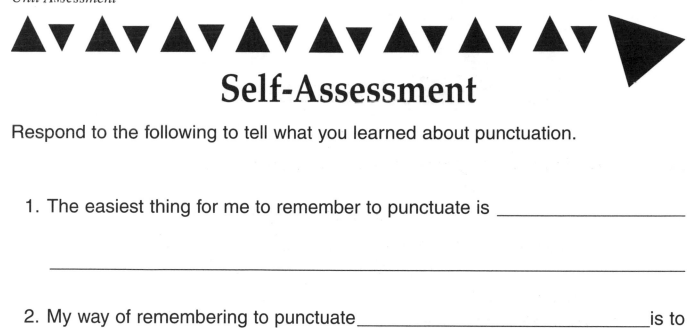

Self-Assessment

Respond to the following to tell what you learned about punctuation.

1. The easiest thing for me to remember to punctuate is _____

    _____

2. My way of remembering to punctuate_____is to

    _____

3. I still have trouble remembering to punctuate _____

    _____

4. When I have trouble remembering what to punctuate, I _____

    _____

5. I'm not sure I understand how or why to punctuate _____

    _____

6. I think I could teach someone else how to punctuate _____

    _____

7. I would be a good teacher because_____

    _____

Punctuation Reference Page

Period

- A period ends declarative sentences. I like chocolate ice cream.
- A period ends imperative sentences. Shut the door.
- A period ends follows most abbreviations. I saw Dr. Swan.
- A series of periods (an ellipsis) shows where words are left out. Four score and seven years ago . . .

Question Mark

- A question mark ends interrogative sentences. When does school start?

Exclamation Point

- An exclamation point ends exclamatory sentences. We won the game!
- An exclamation point follows interjections. Yes! That is the correct answer.

Commas

- Commas separate items in a series. I like blue, yellow, and green.
- Commas separate adjectives describing the same noun. I saw a big, scary cat.
- Commas separate the day and year . Today is March 25, 1999.
- Commas separate the city and state. I was born in Denver, Colorado.
- Commas follow the greeting and closing in a letter. Dear Mike, *and* Truly, Tom
- Commas set off a direct quotation. Tim said, "I ate pizza for dinner."

Colons

- Colons separate the hours and minutes. 7:00

Apostrophe

- An apostrophe forms a contraction. I can't come to the party.
- An apostrophe shows possession. Jane's shoes are new.

Quotation Marks

- Quotation marks surround a direct quote. Mom asked, "Are you ready for bed?"
- Quotation marks enclose chapter, song, and poem titles. We sang "America."

Hip, Hip Hooray!

_____

Knows How to Punctuate!

_____   _____

Teacher's Signature   Date

Ending Punctuation

Use periods after declarative sentences or imperative sentences.

Use question marks after interrogative sentences.

Use exclamation points after exclamatory sentences or after interjections.

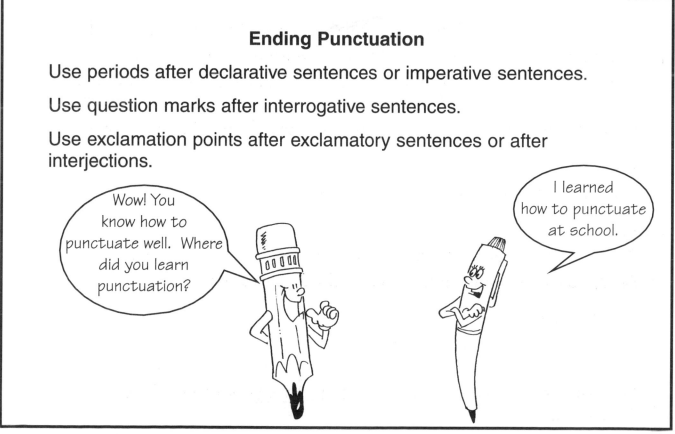

Comma Use

Use commas to separate words in a series or adjectives describing the same noun.

I am happy, proud, and excited to hear it.

I know all about commas. I learned about them from my smart, kind teacher.

Quotation Marks

Use quotation marks to show exactly what people are saying to each other.

A direct quotation is the exact words spoken. Quotation marks are used before and after a direct quotation, and commas are used to set off quotations.

When we write what a person says without showing exact words, we do not use quotation marks.

My teacher says that pens are permanent.

"Pencils are sharp," my teacher said.

46

Answer Key

Page 4
1. .
2. .
3. ?
4. .
5. ?
6. !

Page 7
For all, the question mark should be circled at the end of each sentence.
1. What
2. Where
3. Who
4. Is
5. Why
6. How
7. Do
8. When

Page 12
Each abbreviation should have a period at the end.
1. March
2. Tuesday
3. year
4. feet
5. dozen
6. Doctor
7. page
8. mister
9. Junior
10. yard
11. inch
12. Street

Page 14
1. Jack, be nimble…jump over the candlestick.
2. Jack and Jill went up the hill…Jack fell down…Jill came tumbling after.
3. Mary had a little lamb…And everywhere that Mary went….

Page 15
1. Are you going to come with us?
2. My mom will pick us up from school.
3. Joey gave me a piece of gum.
4. I won!
5. Her favorite color is green.
6. What should I eat for lunch?
7. That is expensive!
8. I need to clean my hamster's cage.
9. What are we going to play at recess?
10. I got an A!

Page 16
1.–4. Check each sentence for the correct use of ending punctuation.
5. dr.
6. st.
7. ft.
8. Mon.
9. dz.
10. p.

Page 17
Items may be listed in any order.
1. pencil, pen, and paper
2. desk, chair, and person
3. TV, phone, and radio
4. socks, shoes, and shirt
5. apple, banana, and orange
6. lion, tiger, and elephant

Page 18
1. I had a sandwich, a banana, and cookies for lunch.
2. Is your favorite color blue, yellow, or red?
3. We saw clowns, acrobats, and elephants at the circus.
4. I like to play soccer, baseball, and hockey.
5. Would you like to use crayons, markers, or pencils to color the picture?
6. Do you want to draw, color, or paint?
7. We went on field trips to the farm, museum, and fire station.
8. Do you want to be a policeman, fireman, or teacher when you grow up?
9. Tom, Neil, Emma, Chad, and Sam each gave me a birthday present.
10. We can have pizza, chicken, hamburgers, or spaghetti for dinner.

Page 20
1. My dog has a wet, pink tongue.
2. Juanita brought a sharp, new, yellow pencil to school.
3. A big, new, shiny car raced past us.
4. The big, hairy, green monster scared me.
5. We play handball with the big, bouncy, red ball.
6. My sister wore old, torn jeans.
7. I like to eat juicy, sweet, red apples.
8. The large, hot, pepperoni pizza was delivered to our house.
9. A tall, bald man knocked on the door.
10. My dad has a long, dark, fuzzy mustache.

Page 22
1. April 15, 2007
2. December 31, 1835
3. February 3, 2010
4. August 10, 1987
5. Feb. 11, 1929
6. Apr. 8, 2000
7. Mar. 16, 2003
8. Sept. 21, 1997

Page 24
1. Boston, Massachusetts
2. Eden Prairie, Minnesota
3. San Francisco, California
4. Tempe, Arizona
5. Roanoke, Virginia
6. Detroit, Michigan
7. Orlando, Florida
8. Youngstown, Ohio
9. Anchorage, AK
10. Boise, ID
11. Newark, NJ
12. Baltimore, MD

Page 26
1. Respectfully,
2. Sincerely,
3. Best wishes,
4. With love,
5. Dear [name],
6. Yours truly,
7. Sincerely yours,
8. Love,

Page 28
1. My brother was born in Denver, Colorado.
2. He was born on December 10, 1985.
3. It was a cold, windy day.
4. He weighed 7 lbs. 6 oz. and was a beautiful baby.
5. My parents named him Alex Jason Solas, or A. J. for short.
6. My grandma, grandpa, aunt, and uncle came to see him in the hospital.
7. We brought him to our house at 525 Main St. after a day in the hospital.
8. He needed a lot of tender, loving care.
9. He also needed lots of blankets, food, and diapers.
10. He started to walk on November 2, 1986.
11. We cheered when A. J. finally walked.

Page 29
April 25, 2000
Dear Mark,
I am writing to invite you to my birthday party. There will be games, food, and cake. I invited all of our friends too. Mark, Cathy, Kevin, and Sam already told me they can come. The information for the party is below.
Location: Jason L. Jones
452 Main St.
Watertown, Illinois 60257
Date: May 7, 2000
I will be celebrating my sixth birthday this year. I hope you can come. It will be a dull, boring party without you.
Love,
Jason

Added 11 commas

Page 30
1. 5:00
2. 7:00
3. 10:00
4. 2:30
5. 9:30
6. 11:30

Answer Key *(cont.)*

Page 30 *(cont.)*
7. 3:00 10. 4:30
8. 11:00 11. 7:30
9. 8:00 12. 9:30

Page 31
1. 2:14 6. 9:50
2. 5:45 7. 2:00
3. 12:15 8. 3:05
4. 2:06 9. 6:45
5. 7:55

Page 32
1. isn't 7. who's
2. let's 8. he's
3. you'll 9. she'll
4. we're 10. you're
5. they've 11. hasn't
6. aren't 12. here's

Page 33
1. they're, o 9. we're, j
2. didn't , i 10. here's, g
3. I've, a 11. mustn't, m
4. I'm l 12. can't, c
5. you're, h 13. I'll, f
6. wouldn't, n 14. 1won't, b
7. let's, k. 15. I'd, d
8. she's, e

Page 34
1. I'm going to the library.
2. She's going to come with me.
3. We're going to look for books about dinosaurs.
4. Let's ask for help.
5. She'll surely help us
6. We've found the perfect book.
7. It's about the types of dinosaurs.
8. I must've forgotten my library card.
9. I'll have to ask you to check it out for me.
10. I promise it'll be turned in on time.

Page 35
1. the girl's doll
2. the elephant's trunk
3. Tom's shoes
4. mom's dinner
5. Sam's sister
6. the principal's office
7. the dog's tail
8. Jake's back pack
9. dad's lawnmower
10. the children's room
1. cat's food
2. bird's nest
3. Miguel's bike
4. Kim's store
5. David's CD player
6. my sister's book

7. my brother's skateboard
8. a baby's toys

Page 36
1. Nicky ran screaming into Manuel's house.
2. My dad knocked down a hornet's nest.
3. I wish I could ride my brother's bike.
4. An alien ate Mariela's homework.
5. Grandpa's spaghetti is the best in the world.

Page 37
1. The doctor said, "You are in good health."
2. Marty said, "My lizard escaped from the cage."
3. He said, "You look nice today."
4. Mrs. Thomas said, "Line up at the door."
5. Dad said, "Come in for dinner."
6. Michael asked, "Can I have a glass of milk?"
7. "Watch out!" screamed Judy.
8. Jason wondered, "Should I go with them?"
9. My sister whispered, "Is the movie almost over?"
10. Mom yelled, "Go, Wildcats, go!"

Page 39
1. Are you going to read the chapter called "The Problem?"
2. We sang a song to the tune of "Old MacDonald Had a Farm."
3. A. A. Milne wrote a poem called "The End."
4. I read an article called "The Octopus."

Page 40
1. 7:00
2. 3:00
3. 5:00
4. can't
5. won't
6. I'd
7. she's
8. they've
9. let's
10. My sister screamed, "It's time to come in for dinner."
11. My family eats dinner at 6:00.
12. Mom said, "I made corn dogs for dinner."
13. They're my favorite.
14. Mom's dinners are the best.
15. Maybe I'll be as good a cook as Mom when I grow up.

Page 41
1 I went to see a movie on Saturday.
2. Wow! You did a good job.
3. How old are you?
4. Sarah finished her homework.
5. Dr. Watson gave me medicine.
6. 12953 Main St. is my address.
7. Mom bought apples, bananas, and pears at the grocery store.
8. I brought scissors, crayons, and a ruler to school.
9. The furry, white rabbit ate a carrot.
10. I flew to Chicago, Illinois, on March 20, 1998.
11. My bedtime is 8:30.
12. Our lunchtime is 12:00.
13. I don't know how to play football.
14. We're ready to go.
15. Let's get popcorn to eat during the movie.

Page 42
Once upon a time there were three little pigs and a big bad wolf. The three little pigs built their houses out of straw, sticks, and bricks. After the houses were built, the wolf went to the pig's house that was made out of straw and said, "Little pig, little pig, let me in." The pig answered, "Not by the hair of my chinny chin chin." The wolf responded, "Then I'll huff and I'll puff and I'll blow your house down." And that is what he did. The house fell down, and the pig ran to his brother's house that was made out of sticks. The wolf went to the pig's house that was made out of sticks and yelled, "Little pig, little pig, let me in." The pig responded, "Not by the hair of my chinny chin chin." The wolf once again said, "Then I'll huff and I'll puff and I'll blow your house down." And that is what he did. The house fell down and the two pigs ran to their brother's house that was made out of bricks. The wolf followed them and said, "Little pig, little pig, let me in." The pig responded, "Not by the hair of my chinny chin chin." The wolf screamed, "Then I'll huff and I'll puff and I'll blow your house down." And he tried to blow the house down, but it wouldn't fall. The wolf made a plan to get into the pig's house by climbing through the chimney. When he finally squeezed down the chimney, he fell into a pot and was cooked for dinner. The three little pigs lived happily ever after.